Make Use of Your Cucumbers!

Popular Recipes to Make Cucumbers a Delicious Part of Any Meal

BY: Nancy Silverman

COPYRIGHT NOTICES

© 2019 Nancy Silverman All Rights Reserved

Subject to the agreement and permission of the author, this Book, in part or in whole, may not be reproduced in any format. This includes but is not limited to electronically, in print, scanning or photocopying.

The opinions, guidelines and suggestions written here are solely those of the Author and are for information purposes only. Every possible measure has been taken by the Author to ensure accuracy but let the Reader be advised that they assume all risk when following information. The Author does not assume any risk in the case of damages, personally or commercially, in the case of misinterpretation or misunderstanding while following any part of the Book.

My Heartfelt Thanks and A Special Reward for Your Purchase!

https://nancy.gr8.com

My heartfelt thanks at purchasing my book and I hope you enjoy it! As a special bonus, you will now be eligible to receive books absolutely free on a weekly basis! Get started by entering your email address in the box above to subscribe. A notification will be emailed to you of my free promotions, no purchase necessary! With little effort, you will be eligible for free and discounted books daily. In addition to this amazing gift, a reminder will be sent 1-2 days before the offer expires to remind you not to miss out. Enter now to start enjoying this special offer!

Table of Contents

Chapter 1. Incredible Cucumber Salads 9

    (1)   Cucumber and Shrimp Salad 10

    (2)   Cool Cucumber Salad 13

    (3)   Cucumber and Beef Salad 15

    (4)   Special Cucumber Salad 18

    (5)   Tasty Cucumber and Beet Salad 20

    (6)   Quick Cucumber Salad 23

    (7)   Cucumber and Chicken Salad 25

    (8)   Cucumber and Dates Salad 28

    (9)   Cucumber and Beans Salad 30

    (10)   Cucumber and Tomato Salad 32

Chapter 2. The Most Delicious Cucumber Appetizers 34

    (1)   Easy and Simple Cucumber Appetizer 35

    (2)   Cucumber Rolls 38

- (3) Cucumber and Salmon Appetizer 41
- (4) The Best Cucumber Sandwiches 43
- (5) Cucumber Cups 45
- (6) Cucumber Bites 48
- (7) Cucumber and Yogurt Dip 50
- (8) Surprising Cucumber Appetizer 52
- (9) Fresh Cucumber Bites 54
- (10) Cucumber and Shrimp Delight 56

Chapter 3. Delicious Pickled Cucumbers 58

- (1) Easy Pickled Cucumbers 59
- (2) So Simple Pickled Cucumbers 61
- (3) Mustard Pickles 63
- (4) Ukrainian Style Pickled Cucumbers 66
- (5) Red Cucumber Pickles 69
- (6) Tasty Bread and Butter Pickles 72

Chapter 4. Learn How to Make the Best Cucumber Soups Ever 75

(1) Cucumber and Tomato Soup................................. 76

(2) Cucumber and Watercress Soup........................... 78

(3) Wonderful Cucumber Soup 81

(4) Cucumber and Goat Cheese Soup 84

(5) Perfect Cucumber Soup... 86

(6) Stuffed Cucumber Soup 89

(7) Simple Cucumber and Potato Soup 92

(8) Cucumber and Egg White Soup 94

(9) Cucumber and Squash Soup 96

(10) Cucumber and Tofu Soup..................................... 99

Chapter 5. Delicious and Easy Cucumber Dessert and Different Drinks Recipes 101

(1) Different Cucumber Cocktail.............................. 102

(2) Cucumber Popsicles... 105

(3) Cucumber and Rosemary Lemonade 107

(4) Cucumber Granita 110

(5) Amazing Hungarian Cucumber Lemonade 112

(6) Cucumber Cake 115

(7) Cucumber Mojito 118

(8) Cucumber Pudding 121

(9) Cucumber Cocktail 124

(10) Delicious Cucumber Pie 126

Chapter 6. Healthy and Super Delicious Cucumber Smoothies
.... 129

(1) Cucumber and Strawberries Smoothie 130

(2) Cucumber and Pineapple Smoothie 132

(3) Special Cucumber Smoothie 134

(4) Cucumber and Apple Smoothie 136

(5) Cucumber and Spinach Smoothie 138

(6) Cucumber and Blueberry Smoothie 140

About the Author.. 142

Author's Afterthoughts... 144

Chapter 1. Incredible Cucumber Salads

If you are in the mood for a wonderful salad for lunch or dinner, than you really need to check out these next recipes! You'll discover the most popular cucumber salads.

(1) Cucumber and Shrimp Salad

This sweet and spicy combination! It's really a great salad!

Prep Time: 15 minutes

Total Prep Time: 15 minutes

Serving Size: 5

Ingredient List:

- 6 Tbsp. Dijon mustard
- 3 Tbsp. white wine vinegar
- 3 Tbsp. white sugar
- 6 Tbsp. homemade mayonnaise
- 4 cucumbers, peeled and cubed
- 1 mango, peeled and cubed
- 3 Tbsp. dill, finely chopped
- 1-pound shrimp, peeled, deveined and already cooked
- Some hot pepper sauces
- 12 lettuce leaves
- Salt to the taste

Instructions:

1. In a bowl, mix sugar with vinegar and stir well until sugar dissolves.

2. Add mayo and mustard, stir well again and keep in the fridge for now.

3. In a salad bowl, mix cucumbers with shrimp, dill and mango.

4. Add salt and hot pepper sauce and stir.

5. Also add dressing you've made and toss to coat.

6. Divide lettuce leaves on serving plates, add cucumber and shrimp salad on top and serve.

(2) Cool Cucumber Salad

It's a simple and flavored salad you should really try!

Prep Time: 10 minutes

Total Prep Time: 1 hour

Serving Size: 8

Ingredient List:

- 4 cucumbers, thinly sliced
- 1 cup white wine vinegar
- 1 white onion, thinly sliced
- 1 Tbsp. dill, dried
- ¾ cup sugar
- ½ cup water

Instructions:

1. In a bowl, mix onion with cucumbers.

2. Heat up a pot over medium high heat, add water, vinegar and sugar, stir well, bring to a boil and take off heat.

3. Pour over cucumber, add dill, stir gently and keep in the fridge for 1 hour before serving.

Enjoy!

(3) Cucumber and Beef Salad

You will find the combination to be exceptional!

Prep Time: 10 minutes

Total Prep Time: 25 minutes

Serving Size: 4

Ingredient List:

- 1-pound beef sirloin
- 1 red onion, thinly sliced
- 1 big cucumber, very thinly sliced with a veggie peeler
- 1 red chili, thinly sliced
- A handful coriander leaves, chopped
- A handful mint leaves, chopped
- 2 ounces peanuts, salted and roughly chopped
- A drizzle of extra virgin olive oil
- Salt and black pepper to the taste

For the salad dressing:

- Juice from 3 lemons
- 1 Tbsp. brown sugar
- 1 Tbsp. fish sauce
- 1 garlic clove, minced

Instructions:

1. Rub beef with some olive oil, season with salt and pepper to the taste, put on heated kitchen grill over medium high heat and cook for 3 minutes on each side.

2. Take off heat, place on a working surface, leave aside for 10 minutes and cut into thin slices.

3. Put beef slices on a platter and add cucumber, chili, onion, mint and coriander on top.

4. In a small bowl, mix lemon juice with fish sauce, sugar and garlic and whisk very well.

5. Pour this over cucumber and beef salad, toss to coat, sprinkle peanuts on top and serve right away.

Enjoy!

(4) Special Cucumber Salad

It's a flavored salad with a special salad dressing!

Prep Time: 10 minutes

Total Prep Time: 10 minutes

Serving Size: 4

Ingredient List:

- 1 big English cucumber, chopped
- 1 avocado, pitted and chopped
- 2 tomatoes, chopped
- 1 Tbsp. lime juice
- 3 Tbsp. extra virgin olive oil
- 2 tsp. tequila
- 1 tsp. herb salad dressing mix

Instructions:

1. In a bowl, mix tomato with avocado and cucumber.

2. In another bowl, mix oil with tequila, lime juice and dressing mix and stir very well.

3. Pour salad dressing over salad, toss to coat and serve.

Enjoy!

(5) Tasty Cucumber and Beet Salad

It's one of the best cucumber salads ever! We can assure you that you'll make it again soon!

Prep Time: 10 minutes

Total Prep Time: 12 minutes

Serving Size: 8

Ingredient List:

- 4 small beets, peeled, cut in halves and thinly sliced
- 1 English cucumber, cut in halves lengthwise and thinly sliced
- 2 small Kirby cucumbers, thinly sliced
- 6 scallions, white and green party sliced in thin strips
- 2 chili peppers, thinly sliced
- Zest from 1 lemon, thinly sliced
- 1 Hungarian chili pepper, thinly sliced
- 5 ounces dry ricotta, salted and crumbled
- 2 cups mixed basil with mint, parsley and cilantro
- ¼ cup white wine vinegar
- 2 tsp. poppy seeds
- A drizzle of olive oil
- ½ tsp. white sugar
- Salt and black pepper to the taste

Instructions:

1. In a salad bowl mix English and Kirby cucumbers with beets, scallions, chili peppers and Hungarian chili pepper, mixed herbs, lemon zest and salted ricotta.

2. In another bowl, mix vinegar with sugar, poppy seeds, salt, pepper and a drizzle of olive oil and stir very well.

3. Pour this over salad, toss to coat, season with more salt and pepper if needed, transfer to plates and serve.

Enjoy!

(6) Quick Cucumber Salad

This will be done in a few minutes! Make sure you have enough for everyone!

Prep Time: 6 minutes

Total Prep Time: 6 minutes

Serving Size: 6

Ingredient List:

- 2 big cucumbers, cut in halves lengthwise and thinly sliced
- ½ cup rice vinegar
- 2 Tbsp. toasted sesame oil
- Sesame seeds, toasted for serving
- Salt and black pepper to the taste

Instructions:

1. In a small bowl, mix vinegar with salt, pepper and sesame oil and stir very well.

2. Put cucumbers in a bowl and mix with sesame seeds.

3. Add salad dressing, toss to coat and serve.

Enjoy!

(7) Cucumber and Chicken Salad

You can make this salad for lunch! You will definitely enjoy it!

Prep Time: 10 minutes

Total Prep Time: 10 minutes

Serving Size: 6

Ingredient List:

- 20 ounces chicken meat, already cooked and chopped
- ½ cup pecans, chopped
- 1 cup green grapes, seedless and cut in halves
- ½ cup celery, chopped
- 11 ounces canned mandarin oranges, drained

For the creamy cucumber salad dressing:

- 1 cup yogurt
- 1 cucumber, finely chopped
- 1 garlic clove, finely chopped
- Salt and white pepper to the taste
- 1 tsp. lemon juice

Instructions:

1. In a bowl, mix cucumber with salt, pepper to the taste, lemon juice, garlic and yogurt and stir very well.

2. In a salad bowl, mix chicken meat with grapes, pecans, oranges and celery.

3. Add cucumber salad dressing, toss to coat and keep in the fridge until you serve it.

Enjoy!

(8) Cucumber and Dates Salad

This is a very healthy salad! Try it and enjoy its taste!

Prep Time: 10 minutes

Total Prep Time: 10 minutes

Serving Size: 4

Ingredient List:

- 2 English cucumbers, chopped
- 8 dates, pitted and sliced
- ¾ cup fennel, thinly sliced
- 2 Tbsp. chives, finely chopped
- ½ cup walnuts, chopped
- 2 Tbsp. lemon juice
- 4 Tbsp. fruity olive oil
- Salt and black pepper to the taste

Instructions:

1. Put cucumber pieces on a paper towel, press well and transfer to a salad bowl.

2. Crush them a bit using a fork.

3. Add dates, fennel, chives and walnuts and stir gently.

4. Add salt, pepper to the taste, lemon juice and the oil, toss to coat and serve right away.

Enjoy!

(9) Cucumber and Beans Salad

You won't need anything else to eat all day!

Prep Time: 10 minutes

Total Prep Time: 10 minutes

Serving Size: 4

Ingredient List:

- 1 big cucumber, cut in chunks
- 15 ounces canned black beans, drained
- 1 cup frozen corn
- 1 cup cherry tomatoes, cut in halves
- 1 small red onion, finely chopped
- 3 Tbsp. extra virgin olive oil
- 4 and ½ tsp. orange marmalade
- 1 tsp. honey
- Salt and black pepper to the taste
- ½ tsp. cumin
- 1 Tbsp. lemon juice

Instructions:

1. In a bowl, mix beans with cucumber, corn, onion and tomatoes.

2. In another bowl, mix marmalade with oil, honey, lemon juice, salt, pepper to the taste and cumin and stir very well.

3. Pour this dressing over salad, toss to coat and serve right away. Enjoy!

(10) Cucumber and Tomato Salad

This is perfect as a side salad for a steak!

Prep Time: 15 minutes

Total Prep Time: 20 minutes

Serving Size: 4

Ingredient List:

- ½ cucumber, diced
- 1 small red onion, thinly sliced
- 1 pound tomatoes, diced
- 2 Tbsp. lemon juice
- Salt and black pepper to the taste
- ¼ cup basil olive oil

Instructions:

1. Put onion in a bowl, add cold water to cover, leave aside for 15 minutes, drain, pat dry and transfer to a salad bowl.

2. Mix onion with tomatoes and cucumbers and stir gently.

3. In a separate bowl, mix oil with lemon juice, salt and pepper and stir well.

4. Pour this over salad, toss to coat well and serve right away.

Enjoy!

Chapter 2. The Most Delicious Cucumber Appetizers

Try each of the appetizers below and make everyone happy! We can assure you that they are easy to make and that they'll taste amazing!

(1) Easy and Simple Cucumber Appetizer

It's so easy to make this amazing appetizer! See for yourself!

Prep Time: 10 minutes

Total Prep Time: 10 minutes

Serving Size: 12

Ingredient List:

- 1 big cucumber, 5/8-inch-thick sliced and seeds scooped out
- Chili powder for garnishing

For the guacamole:

- 2 avocados, pitted, peeled and chopped
- 3 Tbsp. red onion, finely minced
- 1 Tbsp. lime juice
- ¼ cup cilantro, finely chopped
- ¼ tsp. Ancho chili powder
- Salt to the taste
- ½ tsp. green Tabasco sauce

Instructions:

1. Put avocado in a bowl and mash it a bit with a fork.

2. Add lime juice, onion and cilantro and stir well.

3. Also add ¼ tsp. chili powder, salt and Tabasco sauce and stir again well.

4. Arrange cucumber cups on a platter, fill each with guacamole, sprinkle chili powder on top and serve.

(2) Cucumber Rolls

This is a simple cucumber appetizer that will be done in no time!

Prep Time: 10 minutes

Total Prep Time: 10 minutes

Serving Size: 6

Ingredient List:

- 1 big cucumber, thinly sliced lengthwise
- 1 Tbsp. cilantro, finely chopped
- 1 Tbsp. cranberries, dried
- 3.5 ounces canned sardines, drained and flaked
- 3 ounces canned tuna pate
- Salt and black pepper to the taste
- 1 tsp. lemon juice

Instructions:

1. Arrange cucumber slices on a working surface and pat dry them using paper towels.

2. In a bowl, mix sardines with tuna pate, salt and pepper to the taste and lemon juice and stir well.

3. Mash everything using a fork and leave aside for 3-4 minutes.

4. Spoon tuna and sardine mix on each cucumber slice, add cilantro and cranberries on top, roll them and arrange on a platter.

5. Serve right away!

Enjoy!

(3) Cucumber and Salmon Appetizer

If you are in the mood for something more fancy, try this cucumber appetizer!

Prep Time: 7 minutes

Total Prep Time: 7 minutes

Serving Size: 44

Ingredient List:

- 1 big long cucumber, peeled and thinly sliced into 44 pieces
- 2 tsp. lemon juice
- 4 ounces crème fraiche
- 1 tsp. lemon zest, finely grated
- Salt and black pepper to the taste
- 2 tsp. dill, finely chopped
- 4 ounces smoked salmon, cut into 44 strips

Instructions:

1. In a bowl, mix lemon juice with lemon zest, salt, pepper to the taste and crème fraiche and stir well.

2. Arrange cucumber slices on a platter, add salmon strips and ½ tsp. crème fraiche mix on each and sprinkle dill at the end.

Enjoy!

(4) The Best Cucumber Sandwiches

This appetizer is perfect both for a formal party and for a more casual gathering! Try it!

Prep Time: 10 minutes

Total Prep Time: 10 minutes

Serving Size: 12 pieces

Ingredient List:

- 1 cucumber, peeled and sliced
- 8 slices white bread
- 2 Tbsp. soft butter
- 1 Tbsp. chives, finely chopped
- ¼ cup homemade mayonnaise
- 1 tsp. mustard
- Salt and black pepper to the taste

Instructions:

1. Spread butter on one side of each bread slice.

2. Arrange cucumbers on 4 bread slices.

3. In a bowl, mix chives with mayo, mustard, salt and pepper to the taste and stir well.

4. Spread this over cucumbers slices, top with the other 4 buttered bread slices, cut each sandwich in 3 fingers, arrange on a platter and serve right away.

Enjoy!

(5) Cucumber Cups

The filling is absolutely divine!

Prep Time: 10 minutes

Total Prep Time: 10 minutes

Serving Size: 20

Ingredient List:

- 2 big cucumbers, cut into ½ inch thick slices and seeds scooped out
- 2 cups canned chickpeas, drained
- 7 ounces canned red peppers, roasted, drained and finely chopped
- ¼ cup lemon juice
- 1/3 cup tahini
- 1 garlic clove, finely minced
- Salt and black pepper to the taste
- ¼ tsp. cumin
- 3 Tbsp. extra virgin olive oil
- 1 Tbsp. hot water

Instructions:

1. In your food processor, mix red peppers with chickpeas, olive oil, tahini, lemon juice, salt, pepper, garlic, cumin and hot water and blend very well.

2. Arrange cucumber cups on a platter, fill each with chickpeas mix and serve right away.

Enjoy!

(6) Cucumber Bites

This is a classic party appetizer everyone enjoys!

Prep Time: 15 minutes

Total Prep Time: 15 minutes

Serving Size: 12

Ingredient List:

- 12 slices favorite bread
- 2 cucumbers, sliced
- 1/3 cup mayonnaise
- 8 ounces cream cheese
- A pinch of garlic powder
- Salt to the taste
- 1 Tbsp. dill, finely chopped
- Some dill springs for serving

Instructions:

1. Put cucumber slices on a working surface and pat dry them well using paper towels.

2. Cut bread slices in 4 squares each and put them on a plate.

3. In a bowl, mix mayo with cream cheese, salt to the taste, garlic powder and dill and stir well.

4. Add cucumber slices on each bread square, spoon some cream cheese mix, garnish with dill springs and serve.

Enjoy!

(7) Cucumber and Yogurt Dip

This is a Greek party dip also known as tzatziki sauce and it's generally served with pita chips! Try it at your next party!

Prep Time: 1 hour

Total Prep Time: 3 hours

Serving Size: 16

Ingredient List:

- 16 ounces Greek yogurt
- 1 Tbsp. mint leaves, chopped
- 1 big cucumber, peeled and finely grated
- 1 garlic clove, finely chopped
- 1 Tbsp. lemon juice
- Salt and black pepper to the taste
- 1 Tbsp. parsley, finely chopped
- Pita chips

Instructions:

1. Put cucumber on paper towels and leave aside to drain for 2 hours.

2. Put yogurt in a bowl and mix with drained cucumber.

3. Add salt, pepper to the taste, parsley, mint, garlic and lemon juice, stir well, cover and keep in the fridge for 2 hours.

4. Serve with pita chips on the side.

Enjoy!

(8) Surprising Cucumber Appetizer

We recommend you to try this combination soon! It's delicious!

Prep Time: 10 minutes

Total Prep Time: 10 minutes

Serving Size: 10 pieces

Ingredient List:

- 1 big whole wheat tortilla
- 1 small avocado, pitted, peeled and mashed with a fork
- 1 Tbsp. cream cheese
- 2 slices turkey meat, already cooked
- 2 slices favorite cheese
- 1 cucumber, peeled and cut into strips

Instructions:

1. Arrange tortilla on a working surface.

2. Spread cream cheese on it.

3. Also spread mashed avocado.

4. Add turkey slices and cheese slices on top.

5. Add cucumber strips at the end, roll tortilla, cut it into rounds, arrange on a platter and serve.

Enjoy!

(9) Fresh Cucumber Bites

This appetizer is not just tasty! It also looks great!

Prep Time: 10 minutes

Total Prep Time: 10 minutes

Serving Size: 32 pieces

Ingredient List:

- 1 cucumber, sliced in 32 pieces
- 4 radishes, slices in 32 pieces
- 1 tsp. lemon juice
- 2 Tbsp. pecans, chopped
- ½ tsp. lemon zest
- 2 tsp. chives, finely chopped
- 2 Tbsp. mint leaves, finely chopped
- 4 ounces soft cream cheese
- Salt to the taste

Instructions:

1. In a bowl, mix pecans with lemon juice and zest, mint chives, cheese and salt to the taste and stir very well.

2. Arrange cucumber slices on a platter, add radish slices on top, spoon ½ tsp. cream cheese mix on each and serve right away.

Enjoy!

(10) Cucumber and Shrimp Delight

It's a pleasure to share such a simple, yet delicious appetizer with all your loved ones!

Prep Time: 10 minutes

Total Prep Time: 10 minutes

Serving Size: 8

Ingredient List:

- 1 long English cucumber, thinly sliced
- 12 small shrimp, already cooked
- 2 Tbsp. sour cream
- Salt and black pepper to the taste
- 12 whole grain crackers

Instructions:

1. Arrange crackers on a platter.

2. Add cucumber slices on each.

3. Spoon some sour cream over cucumber slices, top each with shrimps, sprinkle salt and pepper all over them and serve right away.

Chapter 3. Delicious Pickled Cucumbers

Who doesn't appreciate some delicious pickles? Therefore, we've gathered the best pickled cucumbers recipes.

Try them all!

(1) Easy Pickled Cucumbers

This is a very easy and fast recipe!

Prep Time: 10 minutes

Total Prep Time: 10 minutes

Serving Size: 4

Ingredient List:

- 1 tsp. salt
- 3 Tbsp. sugar
- 3 cucumbers, peeled and sliced
- 2 Tbsp. vegetable oil
- 3 Tbsp. white wine vinegar
- ¼ tsp. black pepper
- 1 red onion, thinly sliced

Instructions:

1. In a bowl, mix vinegar with sugar, oil, salt and pepper and stir very well.

2. In another bowl, mix onions with cucumber slices.

3. Add vinegar mix, toss to coat, transfer to a jar, close lid and keep in the fridge until you serve it.

Enjoy!

(2) So Simple Pickled Cucumbers

These are so easy to make!

Prep Time: 10 minutes

Total Prep Time: 7 days and 10 minutes

Serving Size: 16

Ingredient List:

- 4 cups cucumbers, sliced
- 1 yellow onion, sliced
- 1 and ½ cups sugar
- ½ tsp. mustard seeds
- ½ tsp. celery seeds
- 1 Tbsp. salt
- ½ tsp. turmeric
- 1 and ½ cups vinegar

Instructions:

1. Divide cucumbers and onion into 2 1 quart jars.

2. In a bowl, mix sugar with vinegar, celery and mustard seeds, salt and turmeric and stir well until salt dissolves.

3. Pour this over cucumber, put lids on and close well and keep in the fridge for 7 days.

Enjoy!

(3) Mustard Pickles

It's a recipe you've probably never tried before!

Prep Time: 20 minutes

Total Prep Time: 10 hours and 20 minutes

Serving Size: 16

Ingredient List:

- 4 cups onions, finely sliced
- 8 big cucumbers, sliced
- 2 Tbsp. salt
- 2 cups sugar
- 2 cups white vinegar
- 2 Tbsp. white flour
- 1 Tbsp. dried turmeric
- 1 Tbsp. mustard powder
- 2 quarts water
- ½ tsp. celery seed

Instructions:

1. Put cucumbers in a bowl, add water to coves, add salt, stir a bit and leave aside for 10 hours.

2. Drain and rinse cucumbers and leave aside for now.

3. Put sugar and flour in a pot and mix with turmeric, vinegar, mustard and celery seed.

4. Stir well, add onions and cucumbers and the water, stir, bring to a boil over medium heat and cook for 10 minutes.

5. Pour this mix into jars, close lid and process in a water bath for 12 minutes.

6. Leave jars aside to cool down and keep them in a cold place until you serve your pickled cucumbers.

(4) Ukrainian Style Pickled Cucumbers

They are delicious! You will eat them in no time!

Prep Time: 15 minutes

Total Prep Time: 4 days and 15 minutes

Serving Size: 40

Ingredient List:

- 5 pounds small cucumbers, soaked in cold water overnight
- ¾ cup salt
- 4 quarts water
- 1 bunch dill stalks
- 1 red chili pepper, thinly sliced
- 1 Tbsp. whole black peppercorns
- 2 garlic heads, cloves separated and peeled

Instructions:

1. Put water in a pot, add the salt, bring to a boil over medium heat and simmer until salt dissolves stirring from time to time.

2. Put some dill stalks on the bottom of a big pickles jar, add half of the garlic, half of the peppercorns and some red chili pepper slices.

3. Arrange cucumbers and then repeat with the rest of the dill, garlic, peppercorns and chili pepper slices.

4. Pour salted water at the end, place a small plate on top of pickles, close jar and keep in a cold place for 4 days.

Enjoy!

(5) Red Cucumber Pickles

These pickles are perfect for holiday meals!

Prep Time: 1 day

Total Prep Time: 2 days 5 hours and 30 minutes

Serving Size: 80

Ingredient List:

- 1 cup pickling lime
- 1 quart water
- 7 pounds cucumbers, peeled, seedless, cut in halves and then sliced
- 2 tsp. red food coloring
- 7 cups sugar
- 3 cups white wine vinegar
- 2 cups water
- 1 tsp. powdered alum
- 1 cup cinnamon red-hot candies
- 4 cinnamon sticks

Instructions:

1. Put 1-quart water in a bowl, add pickling lime and stir until it dissolves.

2. Put cucumber slices in a bowl, add lime water and leave them aside for 1 day.

3. Drain cucumbers, rinse them, put them in a pot and add water to cover them.

4. Leave them aside for 3 hours, drain, rinse and place them in the pot.

5. Add food coloring, alum, 1 cup vinegar and water to cover them.

6. Place them on stove on high heat, bring to a boil, reduce heat to low and simmer for 2 hours.

7. Drain cucumbers, leave aside to cool down and arrange them in a jar.

8. In a pot, mix sugar with 2 cups vinegar, cinnamon candies, cinnamon sticks and 2 cups water.

9. Heat up this mix over medium high heat, pour over cucumbers, close lid and leave aside 1 day.

10. Process jarred cucumbers in a hot water bath for 15 minutes, leave them to cool down and keep in the fridge until you serve them.

Enjoy!

(6) Tasty Bread and Butter Pickles

It's an excellent recipe!

Prep Time: 10 minutes

Total Prep Time: 3 hours and 10 minutes

Serving Size: 50

Ingredient List:

- 6 yellow onions, thinly sliced
- 25 cucumbers, sliced
- 2 green bell peppers, chopped
- 3 garlic cloves, chopped
- 2 Tbsp. mustard seeds
- 5 cups sugar
- ½ tsp. whole cloves
- 1 and ½ tsp. celery seed
- 3 cups cider vinegar
- ½ cup salt
- 1 Tbsp. turmeric

Instructions:

1. Put cucumbers in a bowl and mix with salt, garlic, onions and green peppers and leave aside for 3 hours.

2. Meanwhile, put vinegar in a pot and heat up over medium heat.

3. Add sugar, mustard and celery seeds, turmeric and cloves, stir and bring to a boil.

4. Drain cucumbers, onions and peppers and add to vinegar mix.

5. Take off heat, leave aside for a few minutes, transfer to a pickles jar, close lid and keep in a cold place until serving.

Chapter 4. Learn How to Make the Best Cucumber Soups Ever

Become a star in the kitchen and start making some amazing recipes. Now it's time for you to learn how to prepare the best cucumber soups!

(1) Cucumber and Tomato Soup

It's a lot like a gazpacho and it will taste amazing!

Prep Time: 5 minutes

Total Prep Time: 2 hours and 5 minutes

Serving Size: 4

Ingredient List:

- 4 small cucumbers, peeled and chopped
- 2 onion slices
- 1 and ½ pounds tomatoes, cut in quarters
- 2 garlic cloves, cut in halves
- 2 Tbsp. sherry vinegar
- Salt and white pepper to the taste
- 2 Tbsp. extra virgin olive oil
- Some basil leaves, chopped for serving

Instructions:

1. Put cucumbers, tomatoes, onion, garlic, vinegar and oil in your food processor and blend well until you obtain a puree.

2. Add salt to the taste, stir, pour into soup bowls and sprinkle basil on top.

3. Keep in the fridge for 2 hours before you serve it.

Enjoy!

(2) Cucumber and Watercress Soup

It's what you need after a long and stressful day!

Prep Time: 10 minutes

Total Prep Time: 40 minutes

Serving Size: 4

Ingredient List:

For the soup:

- 3 cups cucumbers, peeled and thinly sliced
- ¼ cups watercress, chopped
- 2 scallions, chopped
- 1 Tbsp. lemon juice
- ¾ cup buttermilk
- ¾ cup Greek yogurt
- 2 Tbsp. white grape juice
- Salt to the taste
- A pinch of cumin powder
- A pinch of cayenne pepper
- Dried red pepper flakes for serving

For the salsa:

- ½ cup cilantro, finely chopped
- 1 tomato, finely chopped
- ¼ white onion, finely chopped
- 1 tsp. jalapeno pepper, minced
- ½ avocado, chopped
- A splash of white wine vinegar
- A drizzle of extra virgin olive oil

Instructions:

1. In your kitchen blender, mix cucumbers with scallions, watercress, lemon juice, yogurt, buttermilk, grape juice, salt to the taste, cumin powder and cayenne pepper and pulse well until you obtain a smooth cream.

2. Add more salt at the end, stir a bit, pour into a bowl and keep in the fridge for 30 minutes.

3. In a small bowl, mix cilantro with tomato, onion, jalapeno, avocado, a drizzle of oil and a splash of white wine vinegar and stir well.

4. Pour soup in soup bowls, sprinkle chili flakes on top and serve with tomato salsa on the side.

Enjoy!

(3) Wonderful Cucumber Soup

It's fresh and you can serve it warm or even cold!

Prep Time: 10 minutes

Total Prep Time: 25 minutes

Serving Size: 4

Ingredient List:

- 2 garlic cloves, finely minced
- 1 Tbsp. lemon juice
- 1 yellow onion, finely chopped
- 1 Tbsp. extra-virgin olive oil
- 4 cups cucumbers, peeled and thinly sliced
- Salt and black pepper to the taste
- 1 avocado, pitted, peeled and chopped
- 1 and ½ cups veggie stock
- ½ cup yogurt
- A pinch of cayenne pepper
- ¼ cup parsley, finely chopped + some more for serving

Instructions:

1. Heat up a pot with the oil over medium high heat, add onion and garlic, stir and cook for 4 minutes.

2. Add lemon juice, stir and cook for 1 more minute.

3. Add 3 and ¾ cups cucumbers, salt, pepper, cayenne pepper and stock, stir, bring to a boil, reduce heat to medium and simmer for 8 minutes.

4. Pour this into your kitchen blender, puree until your obtain a puree.

5. Add parsley and avocado and puree again.

6. Transfer to a big bowl, add yogurt, more salt and pepper to the taste and the rest of the cucumbers.

7. Pour into small soup bowls and serve with parsley sprinkled on top.

Enjoy!

(4) Cucumber and Goat Cheese Soup

It's an unbelievably tasty soup!

Prep Time: 15 minutes

Total Prep Time: 15 minutes

Serving Size: 4

Ingredient List:

- 5.3 ounces goat cheese
- 3 cucumbers, peeled and chopped
- 2 avocados, pitted and chopped
- ¼ cup coconut milk
- Juice from 3 limes
- 1 tsp. cumin
- 1 tsp. Tabasco sauce
- 1 Tbsp. ginger, finely minced
- Salt and white pepper to the taste

Instructions:

1. Put cucumbers and avocados in your food processor and blend very well.

2. Add goat cheese, lime juice, coconut milk, cumin, ginger and Tabasco and pulse a few more times.

3. Add salt and pepper to the taste, pour into soup bowls and chill before serving.

Enjoy!

(5) Perfect Cucumber Soup

This soup is perfect for the summer!

Prep Time: 10 minutes

Total Prep Time: 30 minutes

Serving Size: 10

Ingredient List:

- 4 Tbsp. unsalted butter
- 1 yellow onion, chopped
- 3 cucumbers, chopped
- 1 and ½ quarts chicken stock
- ½ bunch parsley, finely chopped
- ½ bunch chives, chopped
- Juice from 2 lemons
- 7 ounces single cream
- Salt and white pepper to the taste

Instructions:

1. Heat up a pan with the butter over medium high heat, add onions and cook for 5 minutes stirring all the time.

2. Add cucumbers, stir and cook on medium heat for 5 more minutes.

3. Add stock, stir, bring to a boil, season with salt and pepper to the taste and simmer for 5 minutes.

4. Add parsley, chives and lemon juice, stir, cook for 5 minutes, transfer to your blender and pulse until you obtain a puree.

5. Transfer soup to a bowl, leave aside to cool down, add cream and more salt and pepper if needed and stir well.

6. Pour into soup bowls and serve cold.

Enjoy!

(6) Stuffed Cucumber Soup

This is really a very special soup recipe! Try it on a special occasion!

Prep Time: 15 minutes

Total Prep Time: 40 minutes

Serving Size: 4

Ingredient List:

- 2 cucumbers, peeled, each cut in 3 pieces and seeds scooped out
- 8 ounces pork meat, ground
- 3 garlic cloves, finely minced
- ½ cup carrots, thinly sliced
- 1 Tbsp. soy sauce
- 1 tsp. oyster sauce
- Black pepper to the taste
- ¼ tsp. baking powder
- 32 ounces chicken broth
- Cilantro leaves, chopped for serving

Instructions:

1. In a bowl, mix pork meat with garlic, soy sauce, pepper, oyster sauce and baking powder and stir very well.

2. Stuff this mix into cucumbers and secure meat inside with toothpicks.

3. Put broth in a pot and heat it up over medium high heat.

4. Bring to a boil, add carrots and cucumbers and cook for 20 minutes.

5. Take off heat, remove toothpicks, transfer to soup bowls and serve with cilantro sprinkled on top.

Enjoy!

(7) Simple Cucumber and Potato Soup

It's a simple soup but a very healthy and hearty one! Try it!

Prep Time: 10 minutes

Total Prep Time: 25 minutes

Serving Size: 4

Ingredient List:

- 4 potatoes, peeled and chopped
- Salt and white pepper to the taste
- 2 cups water
- 1 big cucumber, peeled and chopped
- 1 cup heavy whipping cram
- ½ cup milk
- 1 green onion, chopped
- 1 Tbsp. dill, finely chopped

Instructions:

1. Put potatoes in a pot, add water to cover and some salt, place on stove on medium high heat, cook until they are soft, drain them, mash them a bit and put them in a pot.

2. Add cucumber, salt and pepper, cream, onion and milk, stir, bring to a boil over medium heat and simmer for 5-6 minutes.

3. Add more salt and pepper if needed and dill, stir and pour into soup bowls.

4. Serve hot or cold. Enjoy!

(8) Cucumber and Egg White Soup

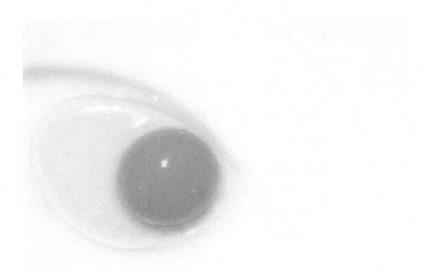

It's a Thai style soup you can make at home when you don't have enough time to cook complex meals!

Prep Time: 10 minutes

Total Prep Time: 20 minutes

Serving Size: 2

Ingredient List:

- 3 ounces cucumber, peeled and chopped
- 2 spring onions, chopped
- 17 ounces veggie stock
- 2 Tbsp. soy sauce
- Black pepper to the taste
- 1 egg white, whisked

Instructions:

1. Put stock in a pot, bring to a boil over medium high heat, add cucumbers and onions and simmer for 5-6 minutes.

2. Add soy sauce and black pepper, stir and cook for 2 minutes.

3. Add whisked egg white, stir very well, pour into soup bowls and serve right away.

Enjoy!

(9) Cucumber and Squash Soup

It's much better that you can imagine! Your family will love this soup!

Prep Time: 10 minutes

Total Prep Time: 45 minutes

Serving Size: 6

Ingredient List:

- 1 big yellow onion, finely chopped
- 3 Tbsp. coconut oil
- A pinch of red chili flakes, dry and crushed
- 4 garlic cloves, finely chopped
- 1 tsp. green curry paste
- 5 cups veggie stock
- 5 big cucumbers, peeled and chopped
- 1 butternut squash, peeled and chopped
- Salt and black pepper to the taste
- 2 handfuls coriander leaves, finely chopped
- 1 cup coconut milk

Instructions:

1. Heat up a pot with the oil over medium high heat, add onion and cook for 4-5 minutes stirring often.

2. Add chili flakes, garlic and curry paste, stir and cook for 2 minutes.

3. Add stock, cucumbers, squash, salt and pepper to the taste, bring to a boil, reduce heat to low, cover pot and simmer for 30 minutes.

4. Take soup off heat, leave aside for 10 minutes, pour into your food processor and blend well.

5. Add almost all the coriander, blend a few more times and return to pot.

6. Add coconut milk reserving a bit for serving, heat up soup again, cook for 3 minutes, season well with salt and pepper and transfer to soup bowls.

7. Serve with coconut milk on top and with reserved chopped coriander sprinkled all over.

Enjoy!

(10) Cucumber and Tofu Soup

This will be ready in only 5 minutes! It's perfect for a busy day!

Prep Time: 5 minutes

Total Prep Time: 5 minutes

Serving Size: 4

Ingredient List:

- 4 small cucumbers, chopped
- 14 ounces soft tofu, drained
- 10 mint leaves, roughly chopped
- Salt and black pepper to the taste
- ¼ tsp. cumin powder
- 2 Tbsp. lemon juice
- 1/3 tsp. ginger, finely grated
- 3 Thai green chilies, chopped
- Water as needed
- 2 Tbsp. salsa for serving

Instructions:

1. In your food processor, mix cucumbers with tofu, mint, cumin, lemon juice, ginger, salt, pepper to the taste, chilies and enough water to give soup consistency.

2. Puree well, transfer to soup bowls and serve with salsa on top.

Enjoy!

Chapter 5. Delicious and Easy Cucumber Dessert and Different Drinks Recipes

This amazing culinary trip end with something really special: cucumber desserts and different cucumber drinks!

You are about to discover some easy and delicious recipes! Pay attention!

(1) Different Cucumber Cocktail

It's something different, refreshing and revitalizing!

Prep Time: 5 minutes

Total Prep Time: 15 minutes

Serving Size: 2

Ingredient List:

- 1 cup cucumber, cut in small chunks
- 4 ounces tequila
- 6 Tbsp. blackberry syrup
- 12 mint leaves
- ¼ cup lemon juice
- Ice
- Cold club soda

For the blackberry syrup:

- 1 cup blackberries
- ½ cup sugar
- ½ cup water

Instructions:

1. Put blackberries in a pot.

2. Add ½ cup sugar and ½ cup water, stir, bring to a boil over medium heat, simmer for 5 minutes, take off heat, strain syrup, discard solids and leave aside to cool down.

3. In your blender, mix cucumber with lemon juice and mint, pulse well and strain this mix into a jar.

4. Put ice in 2 tall glasses and add 2 ounces tequila in each.

5. Add 3 Tbsp. blackberry syrup and 3 Tbsp. cucumber mix in each glass.

6. Top with club soda, stir and serve.

Enjoy!

(2) Cucumber Popsicles

These are perfect for a summer day! It's such a delightful dessert!

Prep Time: 10 minutes

Total Prep Time: 3 hours and 10 minutes

Serving Size: 12

Ingredient List:

- 1 cucumber, chopped
- Juice from ½ lemon
- 1 cup coconut water
- 1 Tbsp. agave nectar
- 1 Tbsp. lemon zest

Instructions:

1. In your blender, mix cucumber with lemon juice, coconut water, lemon zest and agave nectar and pulse very well.

2. Pour into ice lollypop molds and keep in the freezer for about 3 hours before you serve them.

Enjoy!

(3) Cucumber and Rosemary Lemonade

It's a flavored and fresh lemonade you will enjoy for sure!

Prep Time: 5 minutes

Total Prep Time: 5 minutes

Serving Size: 4

Ingredient List:

- 3 cucumbers, sliced
- 1 Tbsp. fresh rosemary, chopped
- 4 rosemary springs for serving
- ½ cup lemon juice
- 3 Tbsp. agave syrup
- 1 cup water
- Ice cubes

Instructions:

1. Take 12 cucumber slices and leave them aside for now.

2. Chop the rest of the cucumbers and put them in your blender.

3. Add rosemary and pulse well.

4. Strain into a bowl, press well, add lemon juice, agave syrup and water and stir well.

5. Pour into glasses, add ice cubes and serve with cucumber slices on top and rosemary springs.

Enjoy!

(4) Cucumber Granita

You only need a few ingredients to make this special dessert!

Prep Time: 10 minutes

Total Prep Time: 3 hours and 10 minutes

Serving Size: 2

Ingredient List:

- 2 cucumbers, peeled, seedless and sliced
- ½ cup sugar
- ½ cup water
- Juice from 2 limes

Instructions:

1. Put water in a pan and heat up over medium heat.

2. Add sugar and bring to a boil stirring all the time until it dissolves.

3. Reduce heat to low and simmer for a few minutes.

4. Take syrup off heat and leave aside to cool down.

5. Put cucumbers and lime juice in your kitchen blender.

6. Add cold syrup, blend well, pour into a dish and freeze for 3 hours before serving it.

Enjoy!

(5) Amazing Hungarian Cucumber Lemonade

It's another very special cucumber drink you can try today!

Prep Time: 5 minutes

Total Prep Time: 5 minutes

Serving Size: 4

Ingredient List:

- 1-quart soda water
- 1 lime, cut in wedges
- 2 lemons, cut in wedges
- 1 cucumber, cut in wedges
- 1 orange, cut in wedges
- Mint leaves
- 3 Tbsp. sugar
- Ice cubes for serving

Instructions:

1. Take 4 lemon, lime and orange wedges and leave aside.

2. Put the rest of the lemon, lime and orange wedges in a pitcher and mix with sugar.

3. Crush the fruits a bit and discard them.

4. Add cucumber wedges, mint and the lemon, lime and orange wedges reserved.

5. Add water, stir and keep in the fridge for 1 hour before serving in glasses filled with ice cubes.

Enjoy!

(6) Cucumber Cake

We think your kids will adore this moist cake!

Prep Time: 10 minutes

Total Prep Time: 1 hour and 10 minutes

Serving Size: 5

Ingredient List:

- 11 ounces white flour
- 14 ounces sugar
- 1 tsp. baking soda
- 1 tsp. baking powder
- 1 tsp. cinnamon
- A handful of mixed almonds and pistachios, finely chopped
- 2 cucumbers, peeled and chopped
- 7 ounces sunflower oil
- 3 eggs, whisked

Instructions:

1. Drain cucumbers well, put them in a bowl and mix well with eggs and oil

2. In another bowl mix flour with sugar, cinnamon, baking powder and soda and stir.

3. Combine the 2 mixtures and stir well.

4. Grease a pan with some oil and coat dust with some flour, pour cake batter in it, introduce in the oven at 320 degrees F and bake for 1 hour.

5. Take cake out of the oven, leave aside to cool down, cut, arrange on a platter and serve.

Enjoy!

(7) Cucumber Mojito

This mojito will hypnotize you!

Prep Time: 10 minutes

Total Prep Time: 4 hours and 10 minutes

Serving Size: 16

Ingredient List:

- 4 cucumbers, peeled and chopped
- 1 and ½ cups agave syrup
- 8 cups water
- ½ bunch mint leaves, chopped
- 1 cup lime juice
- 26 ounces bottle of rum
- 17 ounces sparkling water
- Crushed ice

For serving:

- 1 cucumber, thinly sliced
- Lime wedges
- ½ bunch mint, torn

Instructions:

1. In your blender, mix cucumbers with mint, water, lime juice and agave syrup and pulse until you obtain a smooth mix.

2. Strain, discard solids and pour into a pitcher.

3. Add rum, mix well and keep in the fridge for 4 hours.

4. Pour in tall glasses over crushed ice and serve with sparkling water, cucumber slices, lime wedges and mint on top.

(8) Cucumber Pudding

It's an Indian style pudding you must try today!

Prep Time: 30 minutes

Total Prep Time: 1 hour

Serving Size: 4

Ingredient List:

- 2 cups cucumbers, chopped
- ¼ cup sago
- ¼ cup condensed milk, sweetened
- 1 cup milk
- 2 cups water
- ¼ cup white sugar
- 3 Tbsp. ghee
- 1 tsp. cardamom powder
- 2 Tbsp. raisins
- 3 Tbsp. cashews, chopped

Instructions:

1. Put sago in a bowl, add water and leave aside for 30 minutes.

2. Transfer sago to the bottom of a pan, add water to cover and place on stove on medium heat.

3. When sago is half done, mix with cucumbers.

4. Cook until sago and cucumbers are done and mix with milk, condensed milk and sugar.

5. Stir and simmer for 5 minutes until sugar dissolves.

6. Add cardamom and take off heat.

7. Meanwhile, heat up the ghee in a pan over medium high heat.

8. Add raisins and cashews, stir and take off heat.

9. Add this over cucumber pudding and serve right away!

Enjoy!

(9) Cucumber Cocktail

It's a simple cocktail for you to enjoy on a special night!

Prep Time: 7 minutes

Total Prep Time: 7 minutes

Serving Size: 1

Ingredient List:

- 3 Tbsp. gin
- 4 ounces tonic water
- ¼ lime, thinly sliced
- 6 cucumber slices
- 1 Tbsp. sugar
- 6 mint leaves, torn
- Ice cubes

Instructions:

1. Put mint, gin, sugar and lime in your shaker and mix a bit.

2. Add cucumber and shake again well.

3. Pour this into a cocktail glass, add ice cubes and tonic water, stir a bit, leave aside for 2 minutes and serve.

Enjoy!

(10) Delicious Cucumber Pie

It's a sweet dessert for you to enjoy with your loved ones!

Prep Time: 10 minutes

Total Prep Time: 1 hour and 30 minutes

Serving Size: 5

Ingredient List:

- ¾ cup milk
- 2 eggs, whisked
- 2/3 cup sugar
- 2 cups cucumbers, chopped
- ½ tsp. allspice, ground
- 1 tsp. cinnamon powder
- ¼ tsp. nutmeg, ground
- ¼ tsp. ginger, grated
- 1 already made pie crust

Instructions:

1. Put cucumbers in a pot, add water to cover and then bring to a boil over the medium-high heat.

2. Reduce heat to medium low, cook for 20 minutes, drain and transfer to your blender.

3. Pulse a few times and transfer to a bowl.

4. Add milk, eggs, sugar, allspice, cinnamon, nutmeg and ginger and stir very well.

5. Pour this into pie crust, introduce in preheated oven at 350 degrees F and bake for 1 hour.

6. Take pie out of the oven and leave aside for a few minutes before cutting and serving it.

Enjoy!

Chapter 6. Healthy and Super Delicious Cucumber Smoothies

||||||||||||||||||||||||||||||||||||||||||||||||||||||

Smoothies are so delicious and the best thing about them is that you can even bring them with you at work. They are packed with vitamins and other healthy elements. Try these next cucumber smoothies at once!

(1) Cucumber and Strawberries Smoothie

It's fresh and tasty!

Prep Time: 5 minutes

Total Prep Time: 5 minutes

Serving Size: 2

Ingredient List:

- 1 and ½ cups frozen strawberries
- 1 cup almond milk
- ½ English cucumber, seedless and chopped
- 2 Tbsp. honey
- 1 Tbsp. lemon juice

Instructions:

1. In your kitchen blender, mix cucumber with strawberries, almond milk, lemon juice and honey and pulse until you obtain a smooth cream.

2. Transfer to glasses and serve right away.

Enjoy!

(2) Cucumber and Pineapple Smoothie

It's so flavored and it looks great too!

Prep Time: 5 minutes

Total Prep Time: 5 minutes

Serving Size: 1

Ingredient List:

- 1 cup pineapple, cubed
- ½ cup cucumber, sliced
- ½ frozen banana, chopped
- ¼ cup coconut milk
- ½ cup water
- 1 tsp. lime zest
- 2 Tbsp. lime juice
- A handful kale leaves
- 4 ice cubes

Instructions:

1. In your kitchen blender, mix cucumber with banana, pineapple, coconut milk, water, lime zest and juice, kale and ice cubes and pulse until you obtain a creamy mix.

2. Pour into a tall glass and serve right away.

Enjoy!

(3) Special Cucumber Smoothie

It has such a great taste! We love this cucumber smoothie!

Prep Time: 5 minutes

Total Prep Time: 5 minutes

Serving Size: 2

Ingredient List:

- 1 cucumber, sliced
- A handful spinach
- 1 apple, chopped
- 1 Tbsp. ginger, grated
- 1 Tbsp. maple syrup
- Juice from 1 lime
- 1 cup water
- Some raw bee pollen

||||||||||||||||||||||||||||||||||||||||||||||||||||

Instructions:

1. In your blender, mix cucumber with spinach, apple, ginger, lime juice, maple syrup and water and pulse very well.

2. Pour into a glass, sprinkle bee pollen on top and serve.

Enjoy!

(4) Cucumber and Apple Smoothie

It will soon become one of your favorite smoothies!

Prep Time: 2 minutes

Total Prep Time: 2 minutes

Serving Size: 2

Ingredient List:

- 1 cup cucumber, peeled, seeded and chopped
- ¼ cup water
- 1/3 cup frozen apple juice
- ¼ cup mint leaves, chopped
- 10 ice cubes

Instructions:

1. In your blender, mix frozen apple juice with cucumbers, water, mint and ice cubes and pulse for 2 minutes.

2. Transfer to glasses and serve right away!

Enjoy!

(5) Cucumber and Spinach Smoothie

This is a great smoothie you can enjoy at the office!

Prep Time: 6 minutes

Total Prep Time: 6 minutes

Serving Size: 1

Ingredient List:

- 1 medium cucumber, peeled and chopped
- ¾ cup spinach leaves
- 1 scoop hemp protein powder
- ½ green apple, chopped
- 1 cup water

Instructions:

1. Mix cucumber with spinach, apple, protein powder and water in your blender and pulse very well.

2. Transfer to a glass and serve.

Enjoy!

(6) Cucumber and Blueberry Smoothie

It's a quick cucumber smoothie you can have when you are on a diet!

Prep Time: 5 minutes

Total Prep Time: 5 minutes

Serving Size: 3

Ingredient List:

- 2 big cucumbers, peeled and chopped
- 1 Tbsp. lemon juice
- 1 cup coconut milk
- 1 cup blueberries, frozen

Instructions:

1. In your blender, mix cucumbers with blueberries and lemon juice and pulse a few times.

2. Add coconut milk, blend well, pour into glasses and serve right away.

Enjoy!

About the Author

Nancy Silverman is an accomplished chef from Essex, Vermont. Armed with her degree in Nutrition and Food Sciences from the University of Vermont, Nancy has excelled at creating e-books that contain healthy and delicious meals that anyone can make and everyone can enjoy. She improved her cooking skills at the New England Culinary Institute in Montpelier Vermont and she has been working at perfecting her culinary style since graduation. She claims that her life's work is always a work in progress and she only hopes to be an inspiration to aspiring chefs everywhere.

Her greatest joy is cooking in her modern kitchen with her family and creating inspiring and delicious meals. She often says that she has perfected her signature dishes based on her family's critique of each and every one.

Nancy has her own catering company and has also been fortunate enough to be head chef at some of Vermont's most exclusive restaurants. When a friend suggested she share some of her outstanding signature dishes, she decided to add cookbook author to her repertoire of personal achievements. Being a technological savvy woman, she felt the e-book realm would be a better fit and soon she had her first cookbook available online. As of today, Nancy has sold over 1,000 e-books and has shared her culinary experiences and brilliant recipes with people from all over the world! She plans on expanding into self-help books and dietary cookbooks, so stayed tuned!

Author's Afterthoughts

Thank you for making the decision to invest in one of my cookbooks! I cherish all my readers and hope you find joy in preparing these meals as I have.

There are so many books available and I am truly grateful that you decided to buy this one and follow it from beginning to end.

I love hearing from my readers on what they thought of this book and any value they received from reading it. As a personal favor, I would appreciate any feedback you can give in the form of a review on Amazon and please be honest! This kind of support will help others make an informed choice on and will help me tremendously in producing the best quality books possible.

My most heartfelt thanks,

Nancy Silverman

If you're interested in more of my books, be sure to follow my author page on Amazon (can be found on the link Bellow) or scan the QR-Code.

https://www.amazon.com/author/nancy-silverman

Made in the USA
Las Vegas, NV
28 February 2023